# I'm Going To READ!™

CONSONANTS AND LONG VOWELS

# Long Vowels

STERLING CHILDREN'S BOOKS
New York

In this book you will learn to read these words.
They have long vowels.

# Long **a**

brain cake cane crane day
gray hay pail plane plate play
rain sail snail snake tail train
vase whale

# Long **e**

bee beet cheese deep deer feet
green jeep keep key knee leaf
meet pea queen seal see seed
sheep teeth tree weed wheel

# Long **i**

bike bright dice dive five hide
hive ice kite light like lines
mice pie rhino rice ride right
sign slide spider tiger white

# Long **o**

boat bone coat cold crow ghost
goat gold grow mole nose note
phone piano rose show soap
sold those throat yo-yo

# Long **u**

blue bugle clue cube cute
dune flute fruit fuse glue huge
juice lute mule music ruler suit
tuba tube tune use

# Vowels

## Trace and write.

ghost

A

E

I

O

U

bee

hay

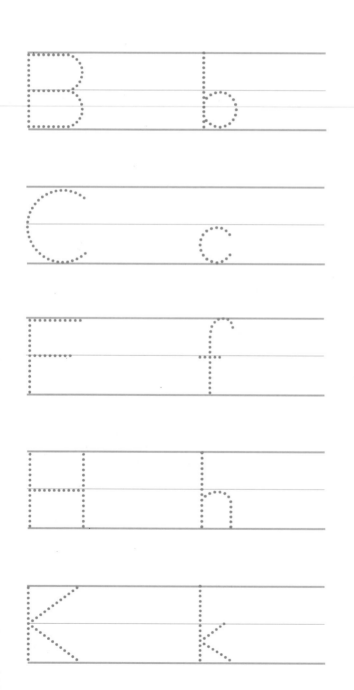

# Consonants

Trace and write.

B b

bee

C c    D d

E f    G g

H h    J j

K k    L l

M m m

N n

P p

O q

R r

S s

I t

V v

W w

X x

Y y

Z z

ghost

# Long a

cane

cake

## Trace and write.

a a

cane

hay

vase

hay     snail     vase

# Writing Words

## Long  a

Trace and write.

plane

train

plate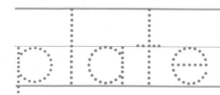

 snake

whale

rain

sail

tail

 pail

 snail

Long
a

b
c
d
e
f
g
h
i
j
k
l
m
n
o
p
q
r
s
t
u
v
w
x
y
z

# Circle all the words in each row that have a Long **a** like cake.

**snake**

**cat**

**train**

**plane**

**cane**

**apple**

**rat**

**pail**

**hay**

Write the Long **a** words where they belong.

pail

sail

tail

snail

# Rhyming Words

Write the words that rhyme with snail.

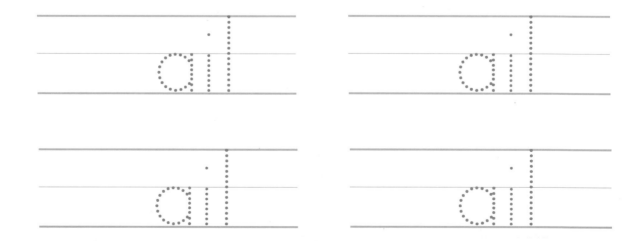

ail

ail

ail

ail

# Word Endings

Read and say these words:

| | | |
|---|---|---|
| cane | train | gray |
| crane | brain | play |
| plane | rain | day |

Write some other words with these endings.

| -ane | -ain | -ay |
|---|---|---|
| _____ | _____ | _____ |
| _____ | _____ | _____ |

Can you write a rhyme?

_____

_____

_____

**REVIEW**

# Long a

Fill in the missing letters to make

Long **a** words.

__ ake

__ nail

__ rain

__ late

__ ail

__ ase

__ lane

__ ay

cak __

mad __

can __

trai __

vas __

ha __

pai __

plan __

# Long

bee

leaf

## Trace and write.

seed

key

pea

key           pea          seed

# Writing Words

## Long **e**

Trace and write.

sheep

seed

deer

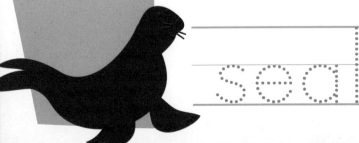

seal

cheese

jeans

wheel

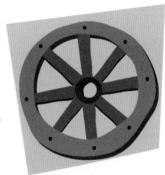

teeth

tree

queen

a b c d

Long
e

f g h i j k l m n o p q r s t u v w x y z

# Circle all the words in each row that have a **Long** like bee.

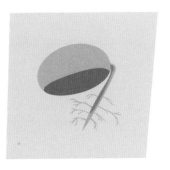

seed

sheep

hen

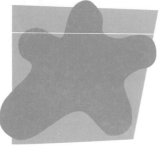

green

bed

jeep

nest

leaf

seal

# Write the Long **e** words where they belong.

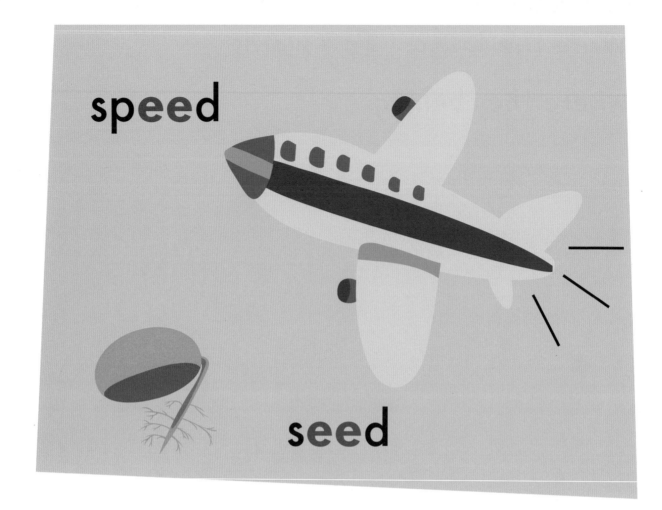

speed

seed

# Rhyming Words

Write the words that rhyme with seed.

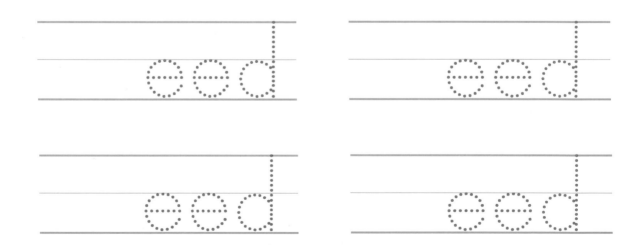

eed    eed

eed    eed

# Word Endings

Read and say these words:

| | | |
|---|---|---|
| bee | feet | jeep |
| see | meet | deep |
| knee | beet | keep |

Write some other words with these endings.

**-ee**                **-eet**                **-eep**

_____      _____      _____

_____      _____      _____

Can you write a rhyme?

_____

_____

_____

# Long e

Fill in the missing letters to make
**Long**  words.

_ eep

_ ey

_ heel

_ ee

_ ueen

_ ea

_ ree

_ eer

a b c d Long e f g h i j k l m n o p q r s t u v w x y z

jee __

tre __

ke __

be __

pe __

lea __

bea __

sea __

a b c d e f g h Long i j k l m n o p q r s t u v w x y z

# Long i

slide

kite

## Trace and write.

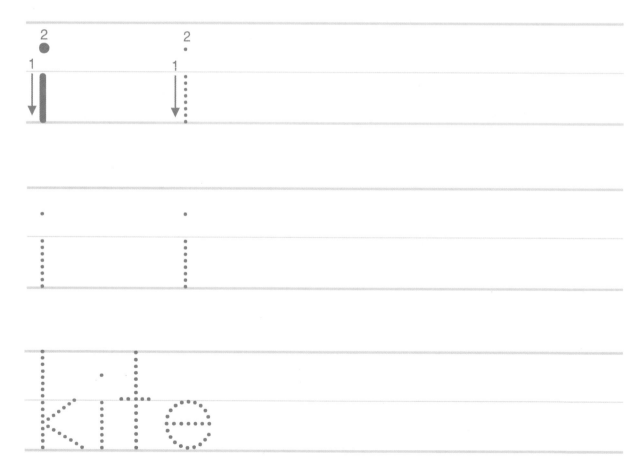

i i

kite

pie

hive

bike

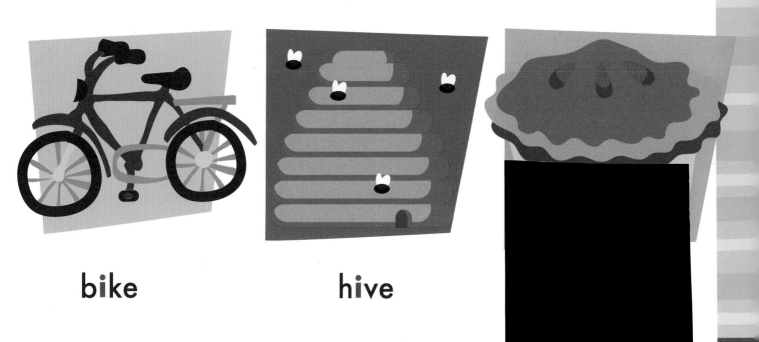

bike          hive

a b c d e f g h i j k l m n o p q r s t u v w x y z

Long i

# Writing Words

# Long

## Trace and write.

spider

sign

lines

slide

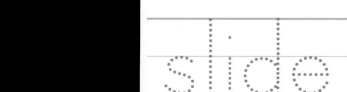

tiger

white

ice

like

 dice

rhino

a b c d e f g h
Long
i
j k l m n o p q r s t u v w x y z

# Circle all the words in each row that have a Long  like bike.

dice

kid

kite

fish

pie

pig

ice

chick

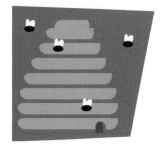

hive

# Write the Long **i** words where they belong.

\_\_ \_\_ \_\_ \_\_

\_\_ \_\_ \_\_ \_\_ \_\_

\_\_ \_\_ \_\_ \_\_

\_\_ \_\_ \_\_ \_\_

a b c d e f g h

**Long i**

j k l m n o p q r s t u v w x y z

dice

rice

ice

mice

# Rhyming Words

Write the words that rhyme with mice.

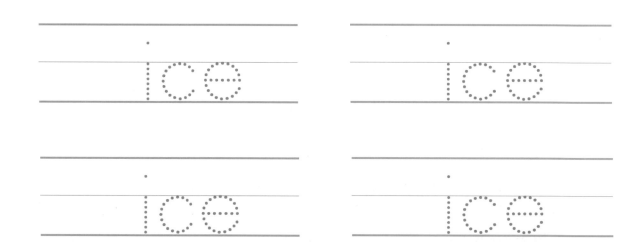

ice            ice

ice            ice

# Word Endings

Read and say these words:

| | | |
|---|---|---|
| five | light | hide |
| hive | right | slide |
| dive | bright | ride |

Write some other words with these endings.

-ive        -ight        -ide

_____   _____   _____

_____   _____   _____

Can you write a rhyme?

_____

_____

_____

# Long

Fill in the missing letters to make
Long  words.

__ iger      __ ign

__ lide      __ ive

__ hite      __ ice

__ hino      __ ie

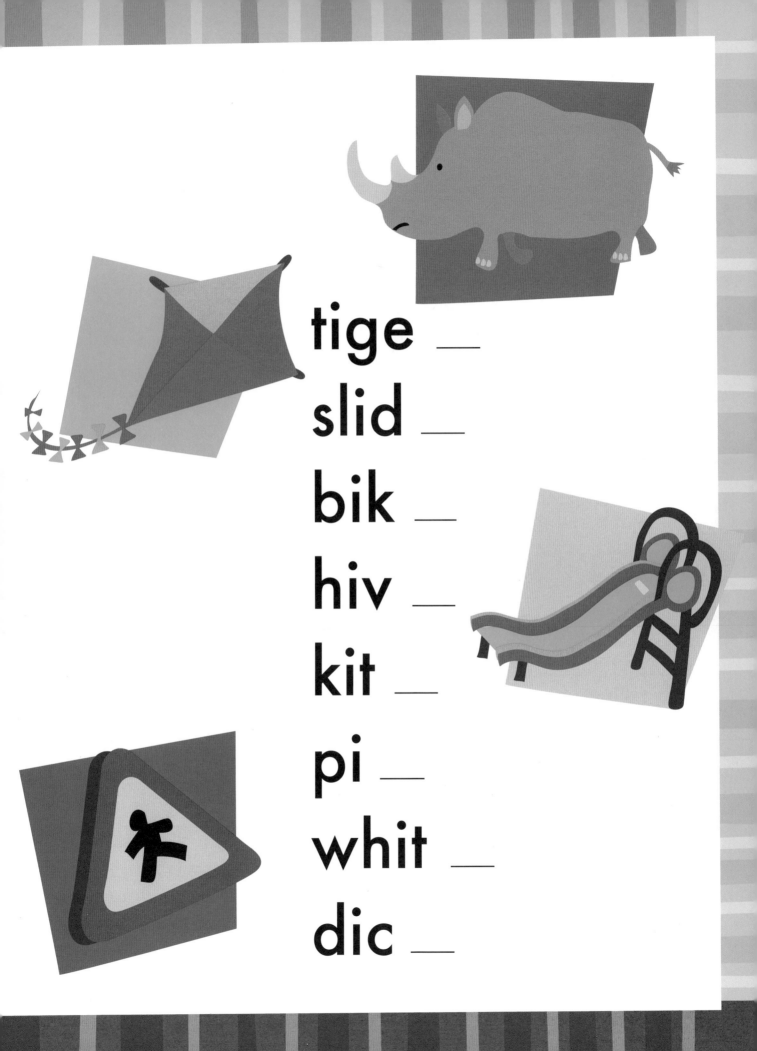

tige __

slid __

bik __

hiv __

kit __

pi __

whit __

dic __

# Long o

phone

yo-yo

Trace and write.

bone

boat

coat

**boat**

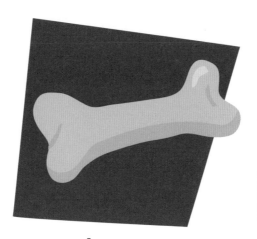
**bone**

**coat**

# Writing Words

# Long o

## Trace and write.

throat

goat

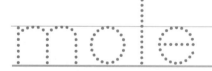

mole

piano

ghost

snow

note

nose

 soap

phone

a
b
c
d
e
f
g
h
i
j
k
l
m
n
Long
o
p
q
r
s
t
u
v
w
x
y
z

# Circle all the words in each row that have a Long  like ghost.

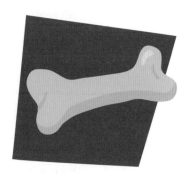

**bone**

**coat**

**dog**

**piano**

**top**

**mole**

**note**

**broom**

**frog**

# Write the Long O words where they belong.

goat

boat

coat

throat

# Rhyming Words

## Write the words that rhyme with boat.

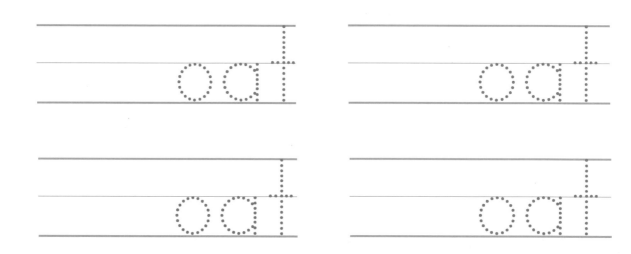

oat          oat

oat          oat

# Word Endings

Read and say these words:

| cold | grow | rose |
|------|------|------|
| gold | show | those |
| sold | crow | nose |

Write some other words with these endings.

-old                  -ow                  -ose

_____    _____    _____

_____    _____    _____

Can you write a rhyme?

_____

_____

_____

## REVIEW

# Long **o**

Fill in the missing letters to make
**Long o words.**

Long

**o**

_ host          _ ote

_ one           _ old

_ hone          _ oat

_ oap           _ oat

not __

soa __

bon __

coa __

goa __

mol __

boa __

ghos __

# Long u

juice

suit

## Trace and write.

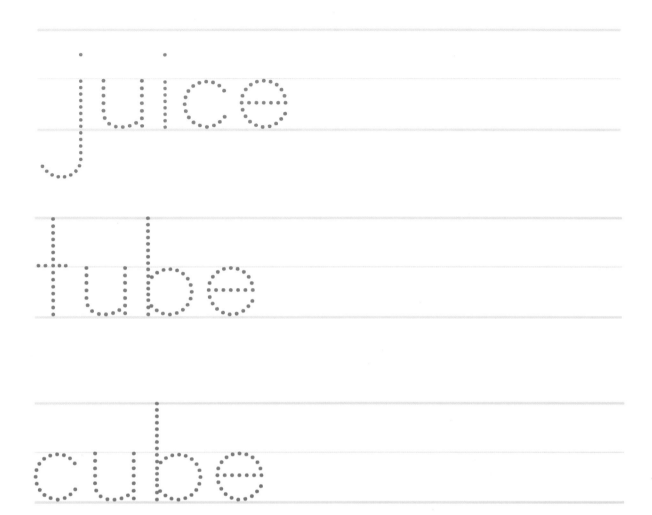

juice

tube

cube

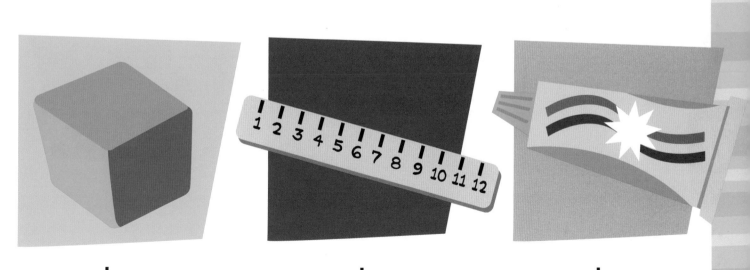

cube     ruler     tube

# Writing Words

## Long 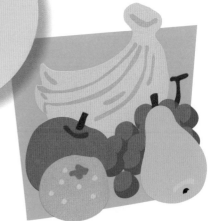U

### Trace and write.

fruit

blue

ruler

juice

flute

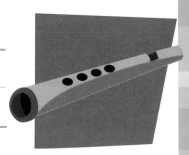

music

bugle

huge

glue

tuba

# Circle all the words in each row that have a Long  u like juice.

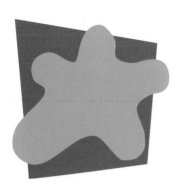

**blue**

**glue**

**truck**

**ruler**

**sun**

**tuba**

**fruit**

**tube**

**duck**

# Write the Long **U** words where they belong.

\_\_\_ \_\_\_ \_\_\_ \_\_\_ \_\_\_

\_\_\_ \_\_\_ \_\_\_ \_\_\_ \_\_\_

\_\_ \_\_ \_\_ \_\_ \_\_

\_\_ \_\_ \_\_ \_\_

a b c d e f g h i j k l m n o p q r s t
Long
u
v w x y z

flute

cute

lute

# Rhyming Words

Write the words that rhyme with flute.

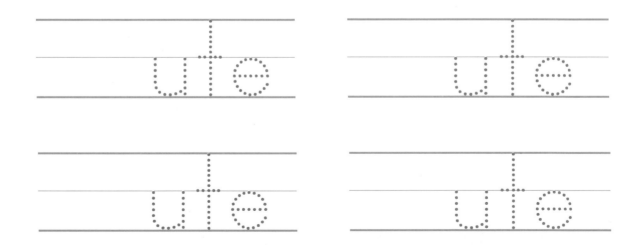

ute

ute

ute

ute

# Word Endings

Read and say these words:

| | | |
|---|---|---|
| glue | dune | use |
| clue | tune | fuse |

Write some other words with these endings.

**-ue**        **-une**        **-use**

_____        _____        _____

_____        _____        _____

Can you write a rhyme?

_____

_____

_____

# Long U

Fill in the missing letters to make Long U words.

__ uice

__ uba

__ ruit

__ uler

__ ube

__ lue

__ lute

__ uge

glu __

blu __

hug __

sui __

cub __

rule __

mul __

tub __

# Long Vowels

Draw a line from the word to its picture.

a b c d e f g h i j k l m n o p q r s t u v w x y z

tiger

blue

fruit

juice

flute

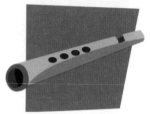

# Long Vowels

Say the word that goes with each picture.
If you hear a long vowel, write down the word.

a
b
c
d
e
f
g
h
i
j
k
l
m
n
o
p
q
r
s
t
u
v
w
x
y
z

## See and say:

## Which words do not have long vowels?

GREAT JOB!

_____

_____
date

_____

_____
first name

_____

_____
last name

★ **I Can READ Long Vowels**